GOODSON MUMBA

Introduction to Management by Harmony

Enhancing Personal and Organizational Performance

Copyright © 2025 by Goodson Mumba

All rights reserved. No part of this publication may be reproduced, stored or transmitted in any form or by any means, electronic, mechanical, photocopying, recording, scanning, or otherwise without written permission from the publisher. It is illegal to copy this book, post it to a website, or distribute it by any other means without permission.

First edition

ISBN: 9798336055313

This book was professionally typeset on Reedsy. Find out more at reedsy.com

Dedication

I extend my sincerest gratitude to my beloved wife, Edith Mumba, and our children, Angelina, Lubuto, Letticia, Lulumbi, and Butusho, for their unwavering support and understanding throughout the conception, writing, and eventual publication of this book, despite the sacrifices and challenges they endured.

Contents

Preface	ii
Acknowledgments	iv
Dedication	v
Disclaimer	vi
Chapter one: The Beach Experience	1
Chapter Two: Organization Redefined	20
Chapter Three: Harmony with the Envitonment	32
Chapter Four: Alignment and Re-alignment	48
Chapter Five: Mastery of Jobs	52
Chapter Six: Ownership of Goals	56
Chapter Seven: Nurturing Internal Relationships	62
Chapter Eight: Yoked Together	67
About the Author	75

Preface

This book primarily focuses on management and highlights how the act of creating humanity reflects the Creator's innate managerial abilities. It argues that principles and laws inherent in creation can enhance organizational management. We recognize that the act of creating and fashioning humanity to oversee the remainder of creation reveals the inherent managerial prowess of the creator. Within creation are embedded principles and natural laws that can refine and elevate management and organizational abilities. While often perceived as a modern discipline, management, as both an art and a process, has been exemplified in creation by its intelligent designer.

Defying simple definition due to its interdisciplinary nature, drawing concepts and principles from fields such as Sociology, Psychology, and Economics, management in this book is delineated as the "art and science of maintaining internal and external organizational harmony to effectively and efficiently handle activities and resources for productivity." This definition resonates with the divine mandate given to humanity by the intelligent designer of creation—to proliferate and extend the essence of the Garden of Eden throughout the world. Humanity was tasked with managing natural resources to replicate the paradise of Eden across the globe.

Genesis 2:5 illuminates this divine imperative further, revealing that prior to the arrival of humanity, no plant had yet sprung forth, and rain had not yet fallen because there was no one to tend to the land. Hence, productivity is invariably contingent upon effective management, and in the absence of sound management, productivity remains elusive.

Jesus Christ and the apostles employed the principles of creation to convey spiritual concepts. For instance, to illustrate the concept of the word of God, Jesus Christ and Peter compared it to a seed, known in Greek as "sperma," from which the English word "sperm" is derived. The intention was to illuminate the unseen aspects of spiritual truths through the principles observed in creation. Just as sperm carries the essence of life and transmits paternal characteristics, so does the word of God serve as the seed from which we are spiritually born, allowing us to partake in His divine nature through the transmission of paternal attributes.

Similarly, the apostle Paul drew parallels by likening the spiritual connection between Christ and the Church to the relationship between a biological body and its head. Just as the human body demonstrates the unseen functional aspects of the head's leadership, so does the Church exemplify Christ's headship. This book introduces a management principle known as Management by Harmony (MBH), rooted in the principles observed in creation. At the core of creation lies the wisdom of God.

Warm regards

Goodson Mumba

Acknowledgments

I wish to express my eternal gratitude to the Almighty God for the boundless wisdom emanating from His universal consciousness, which enriches our understanding of the world. I also extend my heartfelt appreciation to all those who have contributed to my life's journey, providing spiritual, moral, emotional, and material support.

Dedication

I extend my sincerest gratitude to my beloved wife, Edith Mumba, and our children, Angelina, Lubuto, Letticia, Lulumbi, and Butusho, for their unwavering support and understanding throughout the conception, writing, and eventual publication of this book, despite the sacrifices and challenges they endured.

Disclaimer

This book is a work of fiction. Names, characters, businesses, places, events, and incidents are either the products of the author's imagination or used in a fictitious manner. Any resemblance to actual persons, living or dead, or actual events is purely coincidental.

Chapter one: The Beach Experience

Ben is lounging in his customary black trunk, marveling at the beautiful skies while lying on a bed of pillowy soft sand at the Samfya beach. He can feel the sand squishing through his toes as the sun rays bathe him. Alongside him is his wife Betty, who appears to be having a good time tanning in her beloved purple cover-ups and purple sunglasses.

After spending an hour at the beach during the noon hour, Betty advises that the two return to their room to have their lunch. Ben can't believe his eyes when he spots someone engrossed in reading a newspaper while sitting on a beach chair with his legs crossed from around 20 meters away as they make their way back.

"Honey, hold on a second, am I seeing right or are my eyes being deceived? Professor Miller isn't he over there?" Ben questions.

Betty ponders, "Hmm, my dear, what might that elderly gentleman be doing in this place? Don't start imagining things."

Evidently, he is wearing the exact same hat as he did while we were together at Chaminuka Lodge, so I can't miss him.

Betty remarks, "I guess it isn't a bad idea to get closer and assuage your suspicion."

Ben moves in closer and is certain that it is the elderly man himself. This raises Ben's curiosity about what the Professor was doing at the resort.

Professor, what a coincidence. Is that really you I'm looking at? I can't believe it.

How are you, Honorable? I know it's you, Ben. What are you doing here?

I was about to ask you that, Professor.

I'm here for a management workshop, where I'm leading the sessions. We're just two days away from wrapping up. And I assume you're here to enjoy some quality time with your charming wife, Betty, am I right?

Yes, Professor, and tomorrow we leave for home. Today is our last day here.

Where is Betty, by the way?

She just went inside, but I'm sure we can find room to come see you when you have some spare time.

On a more serious point, Ben, I'd like to spend a brief period with you back home.

It's always a pleasure for me to spend time with you. Once you are also back home, I will most certainly follow through. However, I'll let you enjoy reading your newspaper for the time being.

OK, honorable. I assume you want to get back to Betty quickly before she feels like the elderly man is invading her personal space once more.

They share a hearty laugh together.

Betty is just about to leave the room when Ben hurriedly enters there.

"Hey honey, not here again with your old man." Betty objects.

"Forgive me, my love. You must have sensed the urgency in my breath as I hurried back, eager to avoid disrupting our

CHAPTER ONE: THE BEACH EXPERIENCE

tender moment… Interestingly, the professor shared similar sentiments about not wanting to intrude on our romantic time together." Ben responds.

Naturally, I am aware that he seems to be a lonely man and would want to take advantage of any chance to interact, especially with you, I suppose.

Indeed, you're correct. The elderly gentleman lost his wife nearly twenty-five years ago, and most of his children reside abroad, except for the gentleman who serves as one of the directors in his company.

"What is the name of his company once more?" inquires Betty.

Spencer Agro-processing Company Limited and it is one of the country's thriving industrial firms that serves both domestic and foreign markets. You have probably spotted some of their branded goods at supermarkets. Did you know that their product is one of my favorite jams and is now our household name?

Now which one is it?

Prestigious Jam

"Really! the old dude is brilliant." Betty shouts.

Ah, indeed he is! His mind knows no bounds, forever venturing beyond the confines of convention.

By the way, he contacted me a few weeks ago and requested that I join the company's board of directors, which I appreciated.

Why, my darling, have you never told me about it?

I handle a lot of information every day, so sometimes things slip my mind. But I was definitely planning to mention it to you at some point, since it's a process.

I understand, honey.

The doorbell rings…

"I suppose that may be room service for our lunch." Betty guesses.

When Ben answers the door, it is clear that their lunchroom service has arrived.

"Many thanks, sir." Ben speaks to the man who delivers the lunch.

"You're welcome, sir," the gentleman responds.

Ben asks inquisitively, "Your voice, your face, sounds and looks familiar."

Although you were in the senior class, we were in the same theatre club at Kabulonga Boys, the man explained. My name is Kelvin.

Oh yes!! One and two are now adding up. The person who played the chief induna in our play "The Forgotten Kingdom" Is this true?

Yes, sir. It's me.

It's nice to see you again after all this time. You still look the same.

If it's okay with you, I want to speak with you before you leave.

Ben hesitates to respond, appearing to be waiting for the wife's approval, but when Betty makes a go-ahead sign, he nodded in agreement.

Ben replies, "That's alright, but I trust the discussion isn't too confidential that you can't drop me a clue with my wife around."

"No, it's not. In truth, what I crave is further enlightenment about your tome, 'The Years I Spent in a Week.' Each reading grips me anew, entrancing me with its narrative spell." Kelvin exclaimed passionately.

CHAPTER ONE: THE BEACH EXPERIENCE

"Truly? Your feedback is appreciated. It's quite the stroke of fate, isn't it? The professor's presence could greatly enrich our discourse. I'll inquire if he can join us, particularly this evening, and I'll keep you informed," Ben remarks, his tone charged with anticipation and intrigue.

"I can only spare you no more than two hours of our evening, dear. After all, we're not here for meetings, are we? But worry not, for I trust two hours shall suffice. If you could condense years into a week, surely you can make the most of two hours," Betty interjects with a hint of theatrical flair, her words laden with both pragmatism and whimsy.

Ben erupts into peals of laughter, his mirth echoing through the air with dramatic resonance.

As twilight descends, the trio settles into plush couches in a lavishly adorned lounge, enveloped in the warmth of steaming cups of tea. With an air of ceremony, Ben proceeds to orchestrate the introduction between Kelvin and the esteemed Professor, their identities intertwined in the tapestry of the evening's unfolding drama.

"In what manner may I be of assistance, gentlemen?" inquires the professor, his tone steeped in intrigue and anticipation, as though poised to unveil secrets shrouded in mystery.

"Indeed, Professor, if you could graciously afford us but two hours of your time, we would be greatly indebted. There are matters arising from our documented encounter in the pages of 'The Years I Spent in a Week' that beg further illumination," Ben implores, his words laden with a sense of urgency and reverence for the secrets yet unveiled.

"Let us commence," Ben gestures to Kelvin, igniting the flames of our discourse," urges Ben, his signal carrying the weight of anticipation, as though beckoning forth the opening act of an epic saga.

"Alright! from the annals of the very tome 'The Years I spent in a Week,' I am compelled to seek elucidation on merely three matters," Kelvin responds, his words carrying the weight of an ancient scroll unravelling secrets of the ages.

"Speak forth, my child," the professor interjects, his voice resonating with the wisdom of ages past, as though bestowing a mantle of authority upon Kelvin's words.

"Primarily, you delved into the realms of imagination, expounding on how our very reality mirrors the visage of our imaginations. Yet, how do we reconcile this notion with the practice of faith?" Kelvin embarks upon the discourse, his words dripping with intrigue and philosophical depth.

"A profound inquiry indeed! Allow me to draw from the wisdom of Neville Goddard, who defines faith as 'loyalty to the unseen.' In essence, faith entails steadfastly clinging to one's imagination despite the dictates of external reality, conjuring forth existence from the realm of the unseen, much like the creative act of God Himself. As Jesus taught, 'whatsoever things you desire, when you pray, believe that you receive them, and you shall have them,' indicating the necessity of inhabiting the assumption of fulfilled desires within one's mind.

Reality, then, is not perceived as it is, but rather in accordance with one's assumptions thereof, thus shaping a personalized world mirroring the image of one's assumptions. Faith, as the substance of things hoped for, resides in the unseen image within the imagination, from which all visible manifestations derive their existence. This principle aligns seamlessly with Jesus's proclamation, 'it is done unto you as you believe,' emphasizing the omnipotent influence of belief upon one's life.

CHAPTER ONE: THE BEACH EXPERIENCE

Whether one's beliefs are virtuous or flawed, true or false, the law of belief governs the outcome, as the infinite intelligence operates in harmony with the subconscious beliefs held therein. Indeed, as Job lamented, 'For the thing which I greatly fear comes upon me, and that of which I am afraid befalls me,' explaining the profound impact of subconscious beliefs in manifesting reality." The professor expounds, his words resonating with the weight of ancient wisdom and transcendent truth.

"You must place unwavering trust in the boundless wisdom of the infinite, the very essence of life itself, the divine spark residing within you, and divine guidance bestowed upon you through inspired actions to manifest your imaginings," declares the professor, his words reverberating with the gravity of divine decree.

Once more, scripture proclaims, "it is impossible to please God without faith," underscoring the indispensable role of the divine presence in the process of manifesting one's imagination. In every endeavor, one must place their trust in the omnipotent guidance of the infinite intelligence or divine essence, empowering them to bring their visions to fruition.

The dictum "it is done unto you as you believe" emphasizes the importance of focusing on the end result or the desired state of being, rather than dwelling on the intricacies of the "how question." How are my desires going to be fulfilled? To dwell on the "how question" is to abandon the realm of faith and succumb to the limitations of sensory knowledge confined to the five senses, inevitably leading to frustration.

Similarly, when one petitions in prayer, they are instructed to believe that their request is already fulfilled. How else can one demonstrate this belief except by inhabiting the assumption of their fulfilled desire or imagination?

Ben interjects with a query, pondering, "In discussions surrounding policies, it seems we delve into the intricacies of the "how question" in the management planning process. Yet, you've suggested that we should not fixate on the "how question" when bringing our imaginations to life. How do you reconcile these seemingly disparate approaches?"

The professor's response unfurls like the opening of a grand opera, each word a note in a symphony of wisdom. With measured cadence and profound depth, he elucidates the intricacies of the human experience, weaving a narrative that transcends the mundane and ventures into the realm of the extraordinary.

You see, esteemed colleague, many organizations adhere to the SMART principle in their management planning process. This principle dictates setting goals and objectives that are Specific, Measurable, Achievable, Realistic, and Time-bound. In essence, they operate within the confines of the known and the familiar, seeking comfort in a realm where control is paramount.

However, this approach remains rooted in the empirical and the tangible, focusing on realism and empirical correctness. When dealing with goals that demand empirical evidence and sensory validation, one can indeed discern the intricacies of the "how question" in their planning process.

Conversely, when confronted with goals that lie beyond the realm of the known and the familiar, devoid of empirical evidence, one traverses into the territory of faith. In this realm, the "how question" remains shrouded in mystery, for it is a domain where the unseen reigns supreme. Here, one calls forth existence from the void, initiating the journey from the culmination rather than the inception.

CHAPTER ONE: THE BEACH EXPERIENCE

Actions in this realm are imbued with divine inspiration, as manifestations unfold in ways unforeseen by mortal eyes. In the realm of faith, the orchestration of events transcends human understanding, unfolding as a divine tapestry woven from the threads of the unknown.

Allow me to propose that in times of economic downturn or uncertainty, organizations are beckoned not to retreat into the safety of familiar strategies, but rather to embrace the call to creativity, expansion, and growth by venturing into the realm of the unknown. Challenges, far from signaling a retreat into survival mode, serve as catalysts for innovation and transformation, urging us to explore uncharted territories.

Creativity, I posit, is the offspring of faith. Therefore, organizations would do well to operate from a place of faith, where the unseen is transformed into the seen. While adhering to the SMART framework may afford a sense of control, it is through faith that true innovation and breakthroughs emerge.

Man has long sought dominion over his own destiny, yet it is folly to believe that we can navigate life independently of the divine. Indeed, man is but a vessel through which the divine expresses itself, and our ultimate fulfillment lies in aligning our will with that of the divine.

In essence, faith is indispensable when confronted with the unknown and unfamiliar. However, it is crucial to recognize that what may be unfamiliar to one individual may be well within the realm of familiarity for another. Africa, for instance, need not adhere rigidly to the SMART paradigm to navigate unfamiliar terrain; rather, it must lean on faith to forge ahead into uncharted waters.

If it was through faith that the cosmos was birthed into existence, then faith stands as the ultimate law that bridges the gap between the unseen and the seen, the unknown and the known.

"How then do we reconcile the interplay between faith and sensory perception, for it seems we cannot exist in this physical realm without relying on our senses?" inquires Ben, delving into the intricate balance between the tangible and the intangible.

Sensory knowledge confines itself to the realm of the five senses, tethered to the tangible and the observable—the realm of the seen. Faith, on the other hand, serves as the gateway to the unseen, the realm of infinite possibility and potentiality. It is from this unseen realm that the seen emerges, for the seen is but a manifestation of the unseen.

When navigating the seen, sensory knowledge becomes our guide, providing us with the tools to navigate and understand the physical world around us. However, when it comes to bringing forth the unseen into the seen, it is faith that becomes our compass. Imagination, the realm of the unseen, is made manifest through faith, bridging the gap between potentiality and actuality.

In essence, sensory knowledge allows us to navigate the seen world, while faith empowers us to transcend its limitations and bring forth the unseen into reality. Thus spoke the professor, his words echoing through the hallowed halls of wisdom like a thunderclap in the silence of the night, each syllable pregnant with profound insight and existential truth.

"Ah, what a revelation! The veil has been lifted, and now the nexus between imagination and faith stands clear before me," Kelvin exclaims, his voice ringing out like a triumphant symphony in the cathedral of enlightenment.

Scripture explains, "a man's mind plans his way, but the Lord

CHAPTER ONE: THE BEACH EXPERIENCE

directs his steps and makes them sure," underscoring the divine orchestration that guides our paths. Indeed, the statement "it is done unto you as you believe" suggests a passive role on our part, prompting inquiry into the agent that acts upon our beliefs. It is the infinite creative power inherent within us that breathes life into our beliefs, manifesting them into reality.

As Jesus himself professed, "I can do nothing on my own authority; as I hear, I judge; and my judgment is just, because I seek not my own will but the will of him who sent me," emphasizing the divine agency at work within us. Thus spoke the professor, his words akin to the resonance of ancient whispers echoing through the corridors of time, each utterance laden with the weight of divine revelation and timeless wisdom.

Kelvin, undeterred, proceeds to unveil his second query, delving into the depths of emotional attachment to one's imagined ideas and its profound implications.

The professor embarks on a profound exploration of Kelvin's inquiry, beginning with a clarification of consciousness as the amalgamation of thought and feeling, the very essence of existence itself. He posits that the subconscious mind, devoid of linguistic comprehension, discerns importance through emotional attachment, blurring the lines between imagination and reality.

Consider this: Why do tears flow when you watch a moving film, even when you know it's just actors playing roles? It's because your subconscious doesn't distinguish between reality and fiction. If you're emotionally invested, the experience feels real, and your subconscious reacts accordingly, whether it's tears of joy or sorrow.

Drawing from the example of Jesus, scripture reveals that his endurance of the cross was fueled by the joy set before him, underscoring the principle that emotional attachment precipitates manifestation. Indeed, what one is emotionally attached to inevitably manifests in reality, a timeless truth inherent in the fabric of creation.

The significance of emotional attachment extends to the programming of the subconscious mind, wherein constant visualization fosters a sense of familiarity and ease in the realization of desired outcomes. Mental rehearsals serve as the groundwork for subconscious programming, harnessing the creative intelligence within to orchestrate manifestations.

Consciousness, as the fundamental agent of creation, precedes manifestation, necessitating a state of being aligned with the desired outcome. Jesus's admonition to believe that one has already received underscores the importance of embodying the consciousness of fulfilled desires, wherein thought, and feeling converge in anticipation of manifestation.

In essence, consciousness is the catalyst for manifestation, imbued with the power to transform thought into reality. Thus, the essence of attraction lies not in the pursuit of external desires, but in the cultivation of an internal state aligned with the desired outcome—an axiom epitomized by Jesus's teachings on prayer and belief.

"Ah, it all falls into place, and the example of Jesus crystallizes the understanding," Kelvin responds with a flourish, his voice reverberating with newfound insight and conviction.

"Professor, here's a question that weighs heavily on my mind: how is it that individuals who may not adhere to conventional notions of godliness still manage to thrive creatively?" Kelvin interjects, his words laden with intrigue and a quest for deeper understanding.

"Permit me to embark on a journey of meticulous explanation

through what I term the Myth of All Ages," the professor responds, his tone carrying an air of anticipation and scholarly gravitas as he prepares to unravel the intricacies of his theory.

The notion of a Myth of All Ages suggests a pervasive misconception: that scientific revelation and biblical revelation are inherently conflicting. This misconception has had profound repercussions, particularly in hampering the creative potential of religious folks. Indeed, the world now grapples with the dire consequences of misapplied scientific revelation, which has often resulted in the endangerment of human life and the destabilization of our planet, partly because of this retrogressive myth. Recognizing the intrinsic connection between both viewpoints could result in a deeper comprehension of humanity's duty towards the environment.

Yet, I propose a redefinition of science, not merely as a methodical study of the material world, but as the wisdom, skill, and understanding intricately woven into the fabric of God's creation. Solomon, renowned as the wisest of men, illuminates this perspective, asserting that God founded the earth by wisdom and established the heavens through understanding. In the Hebrew context, wisdom connotes skill, while understanding denotes intelligence, suggesting that God's creative prowess is imbued within the very essence of His creation.

The true significance of scientific revelation lies in its capacity to guide humanity towards harmonious coexistence with the natural world, thereby unlocking its abundant blessings. However, the present global predicament reflects humanity's failure to maintain this harmony, resulting in widespread disharmony and ecological crisis.

It is through the lens of scientific revelation that we uncover the universal and mental laws governing the cosmos, offering insights into the intricacies of creation and the fundamental principles that govern our existence.

Let us delve into Romans 1:17-28 and extract its fundamental truths:

1. In theological discussions, there's a concept of two types of knowledge: Specific Revelation, also known in this context as biblical revelation, discloses God through divine interventions or religious texts, whereas General Revelation discloses God through His creation. However, some might liken General Revelation to Scientific revelation, as it involves gathering facts, theories, and principles that explain the workings of the physical universe, from the tiniest particles to the vast galaxies. While scientific revelation focuses on observable phenomena and verifiable explanations of natural events, and general revelation concerns spiritual insights drawn from natural observation and human conscience, both scientific revelation and general revelation unveil the complexities of God's creation, thus affirming the presence of a divine creator. This perspective suggests that scientific discoveries can deepen one's appreciation for the natural world and strengthen spiritual convictions.

2. In actuality, these two forms of revelation are intricately intertwined. Scientific Revelation mirrors Christ before His incarnation, while Specific Revelation represents Christ after His incarnation. Christ is depicted as the Wisdom and Power of God, as well as the agent of creation, emphasizing His integral role in the fabric of existence.

3. Creation serves as a testament to God's invisible attributes, with His eternal power and divinity manifesting through

His handiwork. Those who lived before Christ's incarnation are held accountable for acknowledging divine authorship and ownership of creation, as revealed through General Revelation. However, instead of recognizing God's creative power inherent in His creation, some had turned to idolatry.

4. The apostle Paul refers to this scientific revelation as Truth, revealed by God Himself within man's inner awareness. Those who grasp this knowledge are empowered to move in the realm of creativity, understanding the universal laws governing creation. The essence of this truth resides in every individual, and those who recognize it flourish in creativity. This foregoing truth explains why individuals who may appear irreligious tend to excel in creativity.

5. Nevertheless, Special/biblical Revelation holds greater efficacy than General/Scientific Revelation, as it facilitates the union of man and God. Through this union, man's awareness expands towards divine union with their source, empowering them to produce abundant creative outcomes. This spiritual connection grants access to divine wisdom, transcending the limitations of scientific revelation.

6. Without acknowledgment of God's ownership and authorship of creation, General Revelation or Scientific Knowledge devolves into vain human wisdom and philosophy, devoid of true blessing and prone to becoming a source of destruction and subject to scientific and philosophical error.

7. In essence, the interplay between Specific and General Revelation underscores the profound interconnectedness of divine and scientific wisdom, guiding humanity towards a deeper understanding of the cosmos and its Creator.

"This elucidation couldn't have been more illuminating. Thank you deeply, Professor," Kelvin remarks with a sense of awe and gratitude, his mind aglow with newfound clarity and understanding.

"At your service, my dear son. The pleasure is truly mine," the professor responds graciously, his words resonating with a profound sense of camaraderie and mentorship.

Albert Einstein once remarked, "Look deep into nature, and then you will understand everything better." From the intricate tapestry of creation, we can glean invaluable insights into the divine attributes, including the art of management. The book of Genesis unveils management as the fundamental principle that precedes productivity. As it is written, God withheld rain from the earth until there was a caretaker to tend to the soil. This underscores the pivotal role of management in the orchestration of productivity.

As I mentioned earlier, Ben, I have authored a book on management, delving into the principle of management by harmony, inspired by the wisdom gleaned from nature's intricate balance. When you return to Lusaka, I propose that we embark on a journey to the Spencer Agro-Processing Company Limited, where we can further explore and shed light on this principle of management by harmony.

But before I bid you rest, Ben, I am eager to hear how you have applied the principles we discussed during that transformative week prior to assuming your current position. Please, enlighten us with your insights and experiences.

"Absolutely, Professor," Ben begins, his voice charged with enthusiasm. "Allow me to share one of the dynamic initiatives we've spearheaded—the Mandatory Bonus Awarding system, or MaBAS. Through a spirited competition spanning all public institutions, MaBAS serves as a catalyst for propagating, instilling, and ingraining our nation's core values and principles into the very fabric of our programs and projects."

Ben's passion fuels his explanation as he continues, "We've recognized the profound impact of employee recognition on motivation. By honoring our employees, we ignite a fire within them, fostering a deep sense of commitment and dedication. A motivated workforce not only embraces their roles wholeheartedly but also goes above and beyond expectations, driving our nation forward."

With unwavering determination, Ben emphasizes, "This program stands as a testament to our unwavering dedication to promoting patriotism, a cornerstone of our national identity."

This program embodies the following series of practices intricately woven into the tapestry of patriotism, each designed to uphold and reinforce our nation's values and principles:

1. Theme Interpretation:

a. National Development Agenda (this theme remains static)
b. Each month, the sub-theme undergoes a transformation, meticulously curated by the relevant line Ministry. Rooted in the National Values and Principles (NVPs) which are: morality and ethics, patriotism and national unity, constitutionalism, human dignity, equity, social justice, equality and non-discrimination, good governance and integrity, and sustainable development.

The best and outstanding interpretation of the theme wins an award.

1. Cleanliness (institutional awards only)

2. Customer Relations
3. Internal Relations
4. Budgetary Adherence (departmental awards only)
5. Creativity and Innovation
6. Self-Supervision

Within this framework, the awards are bestowed across three distinguished categories:

1. Employee Awards
2. Departmental Awards
3. Institutional Awards

Each category serves as a beacon of recognition, illuminating the dedication and excellence demonstrated within our ranks.

The accolades are bestowed with grandeur and distinction, offered on a monthly, quarterly, and annual basis to those who embody the essence of theme interpretation and the esteemed values we hold dear. Our vision extends beyond mere recognition; it is a strategic endeavor to sculpt the minds of our civil servants, moulding them into fervent champions of the National Development Agenda.

With each award, we etch the principles of patriotism deeper into their consciousness, leveraging the power of repetition to engrain our nation's mission within their very souls. But our ambitions transcend the public sector alone; we beckon the private sector to embrace MaBAS, inviting them to partake in our noble pursuit of instilling patriotism at the heart of our society. Together, we forge a legacy of unwavering devotion to our beloved nation."

The professor's voice resonates with approval and admiration.

CHAPTER ONE: THE BEACH EXPERIENCE

"That's truly remarkable, Ben… Congratulations! Alright, gentlemen, the stage is yours now. Go forth and revel in the triumph of your endeavors. The night awaits."

Ben's words echo with gratitude and respect. "Professor, your generosity in granting us this opportunity to converse with you is deeply appreciated. Thank you."

Chapter Two: Organization Redefined

As Ben returns to his ministerial responsibilities, he wastes no time in orchestrating a pivotal addition to his agenda. Tasking his secretary with arranging a visit to the esteemed Spencer Agro-processing company, he seeks a meeting with none other than its CEO, the renowned professor himself.

Recognizing the company's sterling reputation and remarkable achievements in the Zambian manufacturing landscape, Ben is eager to glean insights into their organizational prowess. With a swift phone call to the professor, Ben conveys his intent, informing him that his secretary would soon be reaching out to schedule the appointment.

Ben's voice echoes through the phone, carrying a tone of anticipation and respect. "Good morning, Professor. How does this Monday find you?"

The professor's response resonates with warmth and concern. "I'm well, thank you. And yourself, Honorable? Did your journey from Samfya go smoothly?"

Ben's voice carries an air of determination and purpose. "Absolutely, Professor. Our journey was smooth. I'm calling to inform you that my secretary will be reaching out to arrange a meeting with you."

CHAPTER TWO: ORGANIZATION REDEFINED

The professor's voice resonates with efficiency and readiness. "In fact, she just got off the line. We've managed to secure a slot from Wednesday to Friday," he announces crisply.

"Ah, splendid news, Sir," Ben exclaims with palpable excitement.

As Ben's Day draws to a close, he makes a detour to a nearby supermarket, his mind buzzing with anticipation. With each item he picks off the shelves, he can't help but wonder about the production process behind them, especially those from Spencer Agro-processing Company, the very one he is scheduled to tour.

Wednesday morning arrives with an air of excitement as Ben pulls up to the grand premises of Spencer Agro-processing Company. Stepping out of his vehicle, he can't help but be struck by the sheer magnificence of the buildings and the aura of excellence that surrounds them. He is met by a courteous gentleman, older than himself but exuding warmth and respect. It is clear this man has been briefed about the minister's arrival, sparing Ben the need for introductions as he is ushered towards the CEO's office.

Inside, a poised young lady, the CEO's secretary, rises to greet him with a welcoming smile and a gracious gesture. With a swift call to the CEO, she signals for Ben to proceed into the inner office. "Please, make yourself comfortable, Minister," the professor gestures, motioning towards a plush sofa. As they settle into their seats, the stage is set for what promised to be an enlightening encounter.

The professor's reply echoes through the room like the opening lines of an epic saga: "Welcome to our humble empire…"

Ben's astonishment reverberates in the room as he exclaims, "Good heavens! This place is a marvel of excellence. What an atmosphere for productivity! And that vibrant slogan over there, 'A triumphant and robust organization through a triumphant and robust team,' seems to embody the very essence of the brilliance radiating from every corner and every individual here."

The professor nods emphatically, responding, "Absolutely, honorable…"

Ben interjects with determination, "No need for formalities, Prof. Just call me Ben."

The professor's response carries authority, "No, protocol must be maintained. During official tours, you are to be addressed formally. It's essential for the respect and decorum of the workplace. When it's just us, then I can address you as Ben or even as my son, but not in this context."

Ben responds with intrigue, "I understand your point, professor. Returning to the motto, how did you turn it into such a powerhouse of organizational performance? It's clear you're one of the most dynamic manufacturing companies in the nation."

The professor gestures emphatically, "That's precisely why I invited you here. I wanted you to see firsthand what we've achieved, so you might replicate it in the public sector if possible. A strong, winning team is the backbone of a successful organization. When you change your perspective, everything changes with it. If you were to ask our team how they define and view an organization, you'd understand why we've achieved what we have."

Ben's voice echoes with intrigue, "Professor, are you suggesting that you have a unique interpretation of 'organization,' one that diverges from the conventional understanding?"

The professor's voice carries a weighty resonance as he begins,

CHAPTER TWO: ORGANIZATION REDEFINED

"Ben, our perspective on 'organization' transcends the ordinary. Here, an organization is more than just a physical structure or a set of procedures. It's a dynamic network of intellect, a conduit for the flow of cognitive energy that drives performance. We see employees not merely as bodies, but as minds—repositories of potential and capability.

Skin color, ethnicity, and nationality are inconsequential; what matters is the quality of the intellect they bring to the table. We invest in minds, not just bodies. Because it's the mind that shapes behavior, determines outcomes, and fuels progress. A single malfunctioning mind can disrupt the entire network, leading to underperformance. That's why we prioritize mindset above all else—the true source of resourcefulness and resilience."

Ben's inquiry echoes with urgency as he presses for clarity, "Why does this unique perspective of an organization hold such weight, and how does it elevate performance to new heights?"

As the professor delves deeper into his explanation, the room becomes charged with anticipation. "When you recognize that you're not just hiring bodies but minds, you unlock a profound understanding of organizational dynamics," he begins, his voice carrying a weight of conviction. "It's in this understanding that you can shape the beliefs that form your organizational culture.

A robust organization is built on a bedrock of strong beliefs, which in turn stem from the collective mindset of its members. Positive beliefs act as catalysts for positive behaviors, sparking a cycle of innovation and growth."

He pauses, letting the gravity of his words sink in before continuing, "In this paradigm, challenges aren't obstacles but opportunities. They serve as the negative charge that completes the circuit of creativity. For it's only in the tension between positive and negative that true innovation flourishes. This law of polarity governs not just organizations but the very fabric of existence."

His eyes gleam with passion as he emphasizes, "Creativity isn't a luxury but a necessity for relevance. It's the lifeblood of any organization, the driving force behind its products and services. Without it, an organization stagnates and fades into obscurity. That's why we, as stewards of this mandate, must nurture creativity at every turn."

The weight of his words hangs heavy in the air, underscoring the profound truth he's unveiled.

In a flourish of revelation, the professor continues, "Imagine, if you will, an organization as a finely tuned symphony of intelligence, resonating both within and without. Management, then, becomes the conductor of this symphony, tasked with orchestrating internal and external harmony to unleash the full potential of its resources. No wonder in this organization we define Management as *an art and science of maintaining internal and external organizational harmony for the purpose of handling activities and resources for effective and efficient productivity.*"

He leans forward, his voice reverberating with conviction, "Consider the genesis of our existence, where the divine designer charged humanity with stewardship over the Garden of Eden. In this sacred task, man was called to manage the natural world, to cultivate and nurture its abundance. Genesis itself reveals that without the guiding hand of man, the earth lay barren, waiting for his touch to awaken its dormant potential."

With a sweeping gesture, he draws the parallel, "Just as the gardener tends to his garden, so too must the manager nurture the seeds of productivity. For where there is no management, there can be no fruitful yield. Though the concept of management may seem modern, its roots run deep, woven into the very tapestry of creation by the hand of its intelligent architect."

His words hang in the air, resonating with the weight of timeless wisdom.

Ben, struck by the profundity of the professor's insights, ventures forth with a question burning in his mind. "Your definition of management as an orchestration of harmony both within and without is truly captivating. Is this why you've coined it as 'Management by Harmony'?"

"Exactly"The professor, with an air of authority and anticipation, prepares to unravel the intricate layers of the term "harmony" with eloquence and precision.

The term "harmony," as defined by Collins dictionary, denotes the seamless integration of individual components into a unified whole. Philosophically, harmony embodies the ideal alignment of constituent parts with the entirety, whether within nature, society, or an individual. Every living and non-living entity comprises interrelated elements that collectively form its structure.

The vitality and prosperity of living organisms hinge upon the harmonious interplay of their constituent parts. Any disruption to this equilibrium jeopardizes the entity's integrity and viability. The cosmos operates on the principle of harmony, ensuring its sustained functionality. Any deviation from the predetermined arrangement of its components imperils their coherence and expression.

For instance, human-induced alterations to atmospheric composition have precipitated climate change, imperiling human existence. The Creator's design dictates that harmony is the linchpin of effective expression and existence for all living beings. Among these, the human body stands as the pinnacle of organizational complexity, epitomizing divine intelligence through its intricate anatomical structure.

Its optimal functioning relies on the harmonization of internal elements. Disruptions to this internal harmony manifest as physical ailments, impeding interactions with the external environment. Without alignment with its surroundings, individuals experience discord and disarray. Internal disharmony begets external discord, underscoring the interconnectedness of the individual and their environment.

Ben responds, "Professor, you're pushing the boundaries of my comprehension."

The professor elaborates, "Indeed, Ben. Harmony is about aligning the parts in a way that maximizes their effectiveness and complements each other. It's a fundamental principle for the optimal functioning of all living organisms. No organism exists in isolation; they all rely on interactions with their external environment for survival and prosperity.

This necessitates maintaining both internal and external harmony. Internal harmony pertains to the cohesion of its constituent parts, while external harmony involves positioning itself effectively within its environment. An organization, much like a living organism, is composed of interdependent parts."

Ben inquires, "I presume there are various resources besides human resources in an organization that require proper alignment to achieve harmony. However, how crucial is the human resource in organizational performance?"

The professor begins, "Let me provide you with a historical context of human resource management. Back in the era of industrialization, human resources were often viewed merely as a cost to organizations rather than an indispensable asset crucial for their success. Accounting practices treated human capital as a variable cost, and organizational systems were designed accordingly, focusing on minimizing expenses associated with labor. Little attention was paid to recruiting and developing human resources. However, as competition intensified, organizations began seeking ways to enhance their performance."

"Over time, theories emerged aimed at improving organizational performance, with a shift towards recognizing the importance of human aspects within organizations. This shift was championed by influential sociologists and psychologists such as Abraham Maslow, Elton Mayo, Hugo Munsterberg, Rensis Likert, Douglas McGregor, Frederick Herzberg, Mary Parker Follet, and Chester Barnard. Their contributions laid the groundwork for what is known as the Human Relations and Human Behavioral approaches. These approaches emphasized improving working conditions and understanding human behavior in organizational settings."

"As a result of these developments, Human Resource Management (HRM) emerged as a distinct field of study, focusing on the effective management of human resources to achieve organizational goals. HRM ensures that the interests of both employees and employers are balanced, fostering an environment conducive to optimal performance."

In the ever-evolving landscape of organizational management, a new concept has taken center stage: Strategic Human Resource Management (SHRM). This innovative approach underscores the fusion of strategic planning with the traditional functions of human resource management. Various scholars have offered definitions for SHRM:

"a distinctive approach to employment management which seeks to achieve competitive advantage through the strategic deployment of a highly committed and capable workforce using an array of cultural, structural and personnel techniques." By Storey J

"is concerned with 'seeing the people of the organization as a strategic resource for the achievement of competitive advantage" by Hendry, C and Pettigrew, A

"Strategic HRM focuses on actions that differentiate the firm from its Competitors' " by Purcell, J

"The pattern of planned human resource deployments and activities intended to enable an organization to achieve its goals" by Wright, P M and McMahan, G C

Considerable attention has been devoted to delineating various definitions of Strategic HRM due to the shared principles between Management by Harmony (MBH) and Strategic Human Resource Management (SHRM). The parallels between MBH and SHRM lie in their mutual emphasis on achieving a competitive edge through the strategic alignment and effective utilization of human resources.

Both frameworks underscore the importance of harmonious interaction between human resources and organizational objectives across all levels. Conceptually, MBH incorporates some of the theoretical underpinnings of SHRM aimed at fostering competitive advantage. These include the "fit perspective," which advocates for aligning internal resources and skills with external opportunities.

Additionally, both approaches endorse the adoption of best practices irrespective of context, known as the best practice approach. Furthermore, the "functional perspective" posits that organizations thrive when each department makes a unique and maximal contribution. Lastly, the "economic perspective" views human resources as a distinct and valuable source of competitive advantage.

Nevertheless, MBH prioritizes the preservation of organizational harmony among its individual components, fostering cohesion both internally and externally. It places significant emphasis on attaining complementary advantage rather than merely competitive advantage, achieved through strategic positioning and complementarity within its external environment. The nuanced concept of 'complementary advantage' will become clearer as you engage with other staff members. Management by Harmony is built upon seven foundational principles, as encapsulated by the acrostic word "harmony".

Principles of MBH

The initial trio of principles—harmony, alignment, and realignment—fall within the purview of management's responsibility, concerning the orchestration and execution of these strategies. Conversely, the subsequent pair of principles—mastery of jobs and ownership of goals—pertains to employees' roles and their commitment to these objectives. Lastly, nurturing internal relationships and fostering cohesion represent the cultural fabric defining the organization's identity.

Management by Harmony asserts that optimal organizational performance hinges on internal and external harmony. This begins with cultivating internal harmony, enabling the organization to effectively engage with its external environment. Internal harmony primes the organization to leverage the benefits of external interactions. Its sustained viability rests on its ability to maintain harmony with its external milieu. Consequently, the organization's positioning in its external context directly influences its ability to harness environmental advantages, leading to a synergistic "Harmonic Chain Reaction."

On the contrary, discord within the organization poses a dual threat. Firstly, it undermines internal efficiency and effectiveness. Secondly, when human and other resources are not appropriately aligned and integrated within the organization, operational breakdowns occur. These internal dysfunctions preclude the organization from effectively positioning itself in its external environment. Consequently, it fails to adapt to its external surroundings, impeding its ability to capitalize on opportunities and achieve complementary advantages. MBH characterizes this detrimental sequence as the "disharmonic chain reaction."

I believe we've reached a suitable stopping point for today, my esteemed guest. How does that sound? Tomorrow, we'll delve into discussions with other members of our team.

Ben responds, "Absolutely, Professor. This session has been

enlightening, and I'm already grasping why this organization stands tall. Your philosophical insights into the essence of an organization are truly illuminating. They deepen our understanding of what makes an organization thrive."

Chapter Three: Harmony with the Envitonment

The next day, Ben quickly attends to his office duties before heading to Spencer Agro-processing Company Limited. As he steps onto the premises, he senses an aura of achievement that's undeniably infectious. Welcomed once again by the same gentleman from yesterday, Ben is led to the boardroom, where he finds the professor and five other ladies and gentlemen, all seemingly around his age.

"Welcome, Honorable," the professor greets, his gesture extending warmth and respect. As the five impeccably dressed ladies and gentlemen rise in unison, their demeanor exudes a sense of reverence and hospitality, offering the honorable minister a fitting and gracious welcome.

"Ladies and gentlemen, I trust the esteemed minister needs no formal introduction, as his reputation precedes him. It's likely that some of you have already had the privilege of crossing paths with him on various occasions," the professor remarks, acknowledging the collective familiarity amongst the assembled individuals setting the stage for interaction.

Seated prominently in the chair reserved for the chairperson, the professor proceeds to introduce the five directors with a flourish. "To my left, we have John, the esteemed director of

Human Resources and Harmony. Next to him sits Mirriam, our director of Finance and Accounts. On my far right stands Spencer Jr., our director of Administration and Operations. Beside him is Joyce, the visionary director of Research and Development. And lastly, we have Esther, the dynamic director of Sales and Marketing."

Pausing for a moment to let the introductions sink in, the professor continues, "Ladies and gentlemen, as I mentioned earlier, our honorable guest is here for a tour of duty. I trust John, our Director of Human Resources and Harmony, will ensure that the minister's time with us is both productive and enlightening. For now, let us adjourn and allow John to take the lead."

As the others exit the boardroom, Ben remains seated, his attention now solely focused on John, the director of Human Resources and Harmony, who exudes an aura of confidence and competence.

John extends a warm greeting to the minister, ushering him into the heart of their organization with a gracious welcome.

Ben graciously acknowledges John's warm welcome, noting the vibrant energy and jovial demeanor radiating from all the directors.

John responds with fervor, attributing their collective demeanor to the profound organizational culture forged by robust beliefs. He suggests that every individual's conduct within the organization mirrors these deeply ingrained convictions, fostering a cohesive and dynamic environment.

Ben acknowledges his observation, affirming that he's witnessed firsthand the unity and vibrancy within the organization. He then queries the inclusion of "harmony" in John's position title, seeking to delve deeper into its significance.

John clarifies on the guiding principle of harmony within the organization, elucidating its centrality to their management philosophy. He expounds on the concept of Management by Harmony, emphasizing the pivotal role of ensuring harmony both within and outside the organization. The management is entrusted with the task of fostering internal harmony as a precursor to engaging with the external environment. John analogizes the importance of internal harmony to a unified army preparing for battle, highlighting its essential role in facilitating effective external interactions.

He underscores the interdependence of internal and external activities, illustrating how internal disharmony can impede external endeavors such as product delivery and customer engagement. John asserts that organizations with a competitive edge prioritize and invest in maintaining internal harmony. He stresses the need for continual review and attention to internal harmony, emphasizing its significance to organizational performance.

While management bears the primary responsibility for fostering harmony, John emphasizes the collective involvement of all employees in its creation and maintenance. He concludes by affirming that internal harmony is not only a management prerogative but a fundamental principle crucial to organizational success, deserving dedicated focus and attention.

Conversely, internal disharmony within any organization inevitably yields discernible consequences that undermine its external engagements. Analogous to a body experiencing malfunctioning internal components due to nutritional deficiencies, organizational disharmony manifests as diminished performance, hindering effective interactions with the external environment. Such disharmony precipitates subpar performance, culminating in compromised delivery of products and services to clientele.

Ben remarks, "This is intriguing. But does the organizational structure impact the achievement of organizational harmony?"

John responds, "An excellent inquiry indeed. This is a pivotal question that every newcomer, particularly at the directorate level, inevitably encounters. Upon joining as a director, you undergo a session with the CEO, delving into a 'Systematic Thinking' program. In this program, you are encouraged to always think systematically. The CEO provides a meticulous and outstanding depiction of what a systematically structured organization entails. He often emphasizes, 'Let excellence be your aim, so that even if you fall short, you still resemble it closely.'"

The depiction also vividly portrays what internal harmony entails. Drawing inspiration from the biology and chemistry of the human body, it illustrates that every employee or member of the organization is positioned effectively, creating a harmonious blend of these essential components to form a flawless entirety. It showcases how internal harmony within the body is structured:

- Each component must occupy its designated position to ensure optimal functionality.
- Every component must fulfill its distinct role at the appropriate moment and directed towards the intended recipients.
- Timely transmission of signals from the central nervous system is essential for prompt responses to stimuli.
- Nutrients must be delivered to each component in precise amounts and at the right time.

- Each component must possess internal input and output mechanisms.
- Continuous enhancement of effectiveness is imperative for each component.
- Adequate support must be provided to facilitate the survival and growth of each component.
- The central nervous system must receive timely information from its constituents and provide feedback accordingly.
- The central nervous system must maintain its functionality to prevent mental disorders.
- Clear pathways must facilitate the flow of information to and from the central nervous system.
- Accurate interpretation of received information by the central nervous system is crucial.
- Effective functioning of communication lines between components is essential.

Demonstration of Internal Harmony in the Body

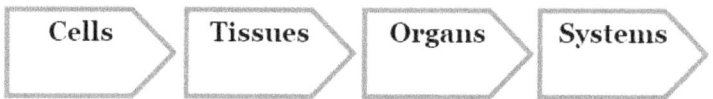

The human body exhibits a remarkable level of complexity and organization, characterized by its intricate anatomy and interrelated systems. Comprising ten distinct body systems, it operates through coordinated efforts among various tissues and organs to fulfill specific physiological functions. These systems collaborate seamlessly to sustain vital processes such as immune defense, nutrient digestion, growth, and reproduction. At its fundamental level, the body consists of individual cells, organized into tissues based on their specialized functions.

These tissues, in turn, assemble to form organs with specific roles, ultimately contributing to larger functional units known as systems. For instance, cells within heart tissues aggregate to form the heart organ, a crucial component of the circulatory system. The comprehensive array of body systems includes the skeletal, nervous, digestive, urinary, lymphatic, circulatory, respiratory, reproductive, endocrine, and immune systems.

The Skeletal System: The human skeletal structure comprises 206 bones, offering robust support and safeguarding internal organs. Bones also serve as reservoirs for calcium, crucial for nerve and muscle cell function. Bone marrow, the inner core of bones, produces red blood cells, specific white blood cells, and blood platelets. Diverse in shape and size, bones are specialized to fulfill distinct roles.

For example, the flat breastbone shields the heart and lungs, while the fused skull bones protect the brain. Smaller wrist and hand bones enhance dexterity, enabling intricate movements, while the long femur in the leg acts as a robust lever for powerful or swift motion. Cartilage, a flexible connective tissue, provides structural support to bones and facilitates joint movement without friction.

The Nervous System: The human nervous system, comprising the central and peripheral components, regulates the functions of all bodily systems. The central nervous system, composed of the brain and spinal cord, coordinates voluntary and involuntary actions. Meanwhile, the peripheral nervous system, comprising a network of nerves, connects the brain and spinal cord to the rest of the body, enabling sensory and motor functions.

The Digestive System: Digestive organs metabolize food into simpler compounds for absorption into the bloodstream and eliminate waste products through excretion.

The Urinary System: The urinary system eliminates waste and maintains water and chemical balance in the body. It includes kidneys, ureters, the bladder, and the urethra.

The Lymphatic System: The lymphatic system collects and transports tissue fluid, aids in fat absorption, removes toxins, and supports immune functions.

The Circulatory System: Blood circulates oxygen, nutrients, and waste products throughout the body, facilitated by arteries, veins, and capillaries.

The Respiratory System: Lungs facilitate gas exchange, delivering oxygen to tissues and expelling carbon dioxide. Air enters through the nose or mouth, passing through the larynx and trachea into the bronchi, eventually reaching the lungs.

The Reproductive System: Responsible for sexual reproduction, the reproductive system comprises germ cells, organs facilitating gamete transport, and accessory glands.

The Endocrine System: Comprising glands that secrete hormones into the bloodstream, the endocrine system regulates metabolic, growth, and developmental processes, as well as emotional behavior.

Ben responds with a tone of awe, "Incredible! But what's the relevance of this detailed illustration to the design and evolution of organizational systems?"

John elucidates, "Extremely significant indeed, honorable. You see, an individual within our organization can be likened to an individual cell, and when individuals with similar functions come together, they form a section, much like cells form tissues. Sections with related functions amalgamate to create departments, akin to organs comprised of tissues.

These departments then coalesce to form systems, similar to how organs with specific functions form systems within the body. Just as various biological systems coalesce to form the human body, an organization is formed from various systems, each with its own objectives and functions.

When one adopts a systematic mindset, every function within the organization becomes crucial, no matter how seemingly insignificant it may appear. This perspective fosters an appreciation and reverence for every role, including that of janitors and cleaners, as they are integral components of the organization's functioning. By recognizing the importance of each function, we inherently treat every employee with dignity and respect. Such values are deeply ingrained in our organizational culture, ensuring that every individual is accorded equal dignity and respect."

Interactions with the External Environment

For survival, sustenance, and growth, the human body must engage with the external environment, obtaining necessary inputs and providing outputs essential for continual health, growth, and longevity. These outputs represent the individual's core competencies, which contribute to addressing societal challenges and are reciprocally rewarded. The nurturing and refinement of these core competencies rely on external environmental inputs.

The fundamental principle underlying this process is the continuous maintenance of internal harmony, serving as the bedrock for societal and ultimately universal harmony. National development hinges on the health of its populace, indicative of a resourceful avenue for progress. National output is contingent upon individual inputs, with internal harmony within bodies facilitating such contributions.

Addressing External Threats

The external environment presents unpredictable and unforeseen challenges that human bodies must confront, often beyond the control of internal mechanisms. These situations can exert a negative influence on the body. The body's response to external stimuli varies based on interpretations by the brain. If perceived as threatening, stress may ensue, leading to adverse reactions such as increased production of harmful substances like hydrochloric acid, which can damage the stomach's mucosal lining. Such instances can disrupt internal harmony and contribute to stress-related disorders.

- **Ulcers:** Slow-healing lesions on the mucous membrane, particularly affecting the lining of the stomach or other parts of the digestive tract.
- **Gastritis:** Inflammation of the mucous membrane lining the stomach.
- **Fibromyalgia:** A disorder characterized by muscle pain, sleep disturbances, and fatigue, often associated with elevated levels of neurotransmitters in the brain.
- **Glaucoma:** A condition marked by abnormally high pressure within the eyeball, leading to damage of the optic nerve.
- **Angina:** A medical condition resulting from inadequate blood supply to the heart, causing severe chest pains.

- **Hypoglycemia:** A medical state characterized by unusually low levels of sugar in the blood.
- **Amenorrhea:** The abnormal absence or suppression of menstruation.
- **Impotence:** The inability of a man to achieve or maintain an erection of the penis.
- **Migraine**: A recurring, intense headache typically affecting one side of the head and sometimes accompanied by vomiting or visual disturbances.
- **Constipation:** Difficulty in passing solid waste from the body, resulting in hard and dry feces.
- **Depression:** A psychiatric disorder characterized by persistent feelings of despair, dejection, poor concentration, lack of energy, sleep disturbances, and, in severe cases, suicidal tendencies.

In an ideal scenario, the goal is to uphold harmony despite external challenges. Sustaining harmony ensures the body retains its resilience to withstand these shocks and lessen their potential impact on internal functions. During times of external threats, achieving harmony is possible when the central nervous system, guided by the mind, interprets external stimuli positively. This interpretation safeguards the body's biological and chemical equilibrium from being compromised.

Ben reflects, "Now it's clear why the Professor likened the human body to the pinnacle of divine organizational prowess. So, how does what you've explained translate to organizational performance?"

John responds, "Here are the key takeaways from the illustration, as imparted by the professor:"

Lessons from Human Body Harmony: The human body

serves as a profound example of Management by Harmony (MBH), as it possesses all the necessary systems to maintain its vitality and resilience. Equipped with mechanisms for self-renewal and healing, the body demonstrates an innate ability to combat external threats and maintain its overall functionality. However, when disharmony disrupts its internal systems, the body's capacity to function optimally and engage with its external environment is compromised.

Similarly, organizations must cultivate internal systems capable of rejuvenating their operations and managing external stressors. Every organization encounters disruptive inputs, whether in the form of materials or information, which can induce organizational stress and disrupt normal functioning. For example, news of potential layoffs may trigger destructive behaviors among employees, leading to operational disruptions such as asset mismanagement.

Internal stressors, often generated by hostile leadership or intimidating work environments, further exacerbate organizational disharmony. These stressors not only affect employees' emotional well-being but also manifest as physiological disorders, impairing their ability to function effectively within the organization.

Central management plays a crucial role in interpreting and managing information to alleviate employee apprehension and maintain a stress-free work environment. By fostering a culture of open communication and support, organizations can mitigate internal discord and promote harmonious functioning among employees.

CHAPTER THREE: HARMONY WITH THE ENVITONMENT

How Organizational Harmony Looks:

- Each employee must be positioned appropriately to ensure efficient and effective functioning.
- Every employee should fulfill their unique role at the right time and for the intended recipients.
- Timely dissemination of information from management is essential for informed decision-making.
- Employees require adequate support at the right time and in suitable quantities to perform their tasks effectively.
- There must be clear channels for both input and output within the organization.
- Employees should continually enhance their efficiency and effectiveness.
- Adequate support should be provided for the survival and development of each employee.
- Management needs to receive timely information from employees and provide feedback promptly for effective decision-making.
- The management itself must be functional and operate smoothly.
- Clear channels of communication must exist between management and employees for effective information flow.
- Management must accurately interpret the information received from employees.
- The communication lines facilitating the exchange of information between employees and management should be operational and efficient.

Dealing with External Threats: Complimentary, not Competitive

Traditionally, competition is viewed as a contest of rivalry where competitors are perceived as threats to one another's operations. However, true competition only exists when opponents share similar goals, strengths, weaknesses, and operational structures, essentially fighting for the same customers.

This implies a scenario where competitors operate within the same parameters, akin to participants in sports categorized by age or weight. For example, in football competitions, teams are grouped according to age to ensure fairness. Similarly, in athletics, marathon runners don't compete against sprinters due to differing strengths and weaknesses.

When participants possess varying strengths and weaknesses, true competition becomes less feasible as some have inherent advantages over others. Simply offering similar products or services does not equate to competition, as differences in organizational cultures and operational methods lead to distinct deliveries.

It is essential for organizations to emphasize their unique features rather than just benefits when marketing their offerings. Each organization is inherently different, akin to individuals, and their prosperity lies in expressing their unique capabilities effectively.

True competition, according to the principle of Management by Harmony (MBH), involves striving to achieve organizational goals and objectives while leveraging the unique mental skills and capabilities of the workforce. While organizations can replicate information resources and technological know-how, they cannot replicate the unique mental skills and capabilities of their workforce. Hence, investing in human resource development is crucial for gaining a competitive edge.

MBH views every organization as a unique entity that thrives on its distinctiveness. Similar to harmonizing voices in music, where different parts blend to create a pleasant sound, organizations should position themselves in a complimentary manner by showcasing their uniqueness. This involves meeting customer needs in a distinctive way through effective utilization of human resources.

MBH sees the efforts of other players as complimentary rather than competitive, advocating for flexible goals and objectives to maintain harmony in dynamic market conditions. Ultimately, differentiation is key to organizational success in interacting with the external environment.

Complimentary Advantage:

Complimentary advantage refers to the edge an organization gains over others by strategically positioning itself in its environment, offering various complementary goods or services, and leveraging them effectively for profit. Management by Harmony (MBH) perceives the environment not as competitive, but as complementary, thus advocating for organizations to strive for uniqueness to secure a significant share in the environment and achieve complimentary advantage. This involves leveraging internal harmony to excel in the external environment.

Dealing with a Recession:

Managing a recession, whether at the governmental or organizational level, requires a holistic approach. Traditionally, organizations have resorted to cost-cutting measures such as layoffs and harsh conditions for remaining employees to mitigate the effects of recession. However, these measures often fail to yield desired results due to the disharmony they create, resulting in underperformance.

In contrast, MBH advocates for maintaining harmony as a remedy to navigate through recession. Just as an ideal state of harmony in the human body ensures optimal functioning, organizations should prioritize meeting the needs of employees to enable them to perform effectively, even in times of crisis. Employees, when well taken care of, are more likely to exert maximum effort to improve organizational performance, akin to the release of adrenaline in emergencies.

While layoffs may sometimes be unavoidable, they should be a last resort and based on performance rather than favoritism. Human capital is a valuable resource that should be preserved, and maintaining internal harmony should be a management priority during recession. Structural adjustments should focus on operational streamlining rather than indiscriminate layoffs.

In teaching on management, Jesus praised a manager who employed MBH principles to navigate a potential job loss due to mismanagement. By harmonizing with both internal and external environments, the manager successfully secured his position and garnered support from both his employer and debtors.

Ben reflects, "I grasp the magnitude of upholding organizational harmony. What resonates with me is the notion that rigidity is simply not an option in this pursuit. Flexibility seems indispensable for sustaining organizational harmony."

John responds, "Absolutely, honorable. It underscores why we continuously adjust and readjust different facets of the organization. Shall we delve deeper into the discourse on alignment and realignment?"

Chapter Four: Alignment and Re-alignment

John begins, "Allow me to share a renowned quote from Professor Igor Ansoff: 'For many firms, periodic, or even continual, strategic repositioning must become a way of life.' This encapsulates our approach as management. We place utmost importance on the alignment and realignment of the organization's various components. Alignment entails bringing individuals or groups into agreement with the policies of others or positioning two objects in a specific relationship. Realignment, on the other hand, is the ongoing responsibility of management to ensure harmony is consistently upheld and integrated into the fabric of our operations."

John continues, "It's imperative to understand that organizations neglecting the process of alignment and realignment do so at their own peril. Harmony within the organization should be prioritized, achievable through aligning and realigning activities with organizational policies and with the employees. Here, we've dedicated a standalone section under my department of Human Resources called Harmony, solely focused on creating and maintaining internal and external harmony.

We acknowledge that misalignment is inevitable in every organization due to various internal and external factors. Just as a human body experiences misalignment primarily due to incorrect consumption or lack of nutrients, organizations face similar challenges. Misalignment isn't always physical; it can be logical when an employee's actions deviate from organizational policies or others' activities. Organizational structures are built on logical relationships among activities. If disharmony arises, management must intervene promptly.

Internal human conflicts also contribute to misalignment, and our Harmony section remains vigilant in detecting and resolving conflicts before they escalate. We have staff certified in conflict resolution to address these issues swiftly and effectively."

Ben queries, "How exactly do you ensure that activities are in alignment with organizational policies?"

John elaborates, "Organizational policies serve as the blueprint for executing organizational objectives. Strategic planning outlines long-term goals, which are then translated into short-term tactical objectives and further interpreted into daily operational activities. Each employee's job description should seamlessly align with the organization's policies, starting with defining the purpose of their position in relation to overall objectives. This purpose dictates the functions of the position, which in turn determine the associated activities and step-by-step instructions.

With the external environment constantly evolving due to technological advancements, organizational performance must be regularly revised to keep pace. As goals and objectives adapt to environmental changes, so should policies. Rigid job descriptions that fail to respond to evolving objectives are a recipe for failure. To ensure alignment between individual activities and organizational policies, constant monitoring and revision of activities are essential, hence the need for a dedicated staff section to maintain harmony.

Continuous change necessitates ongoing realignment of activities. Just as environmental factors evolve, so should organizational activities. This imperative applies not only to profit organizations but also to nonprofits, whose relevance depends on adapting to socio-cultural dynamics. For example, the globalized nature of technology calls for a shift in client interaction methods, prompting internal activity realignment and policy changes.

Organizations that resist change risk losing relevance, regardless of size. Alignment ensures harmony, while misalignment leads to dysfunction and hinders organizational performance.

Ben inquires, "Fascinating insights, indeed. But what about ensuring that employees' activities are aligned and realigned with organizational goals?"

John responds emphatically, "Absolutely, aligning activities with policies is just the beginning. It's equally crucial to ensure that employees are aligned with their respective tasks. The right people need to be matched with the right activities at all times. It's like a puzzle – each piece needs to fit perfectly for the picture to become clear.

Too often, organizations place employees in roles that don't match their skills or abilities, leading to underperformance. But it's not fair to label these employees as incompetent. In reality, they're simply misplaced or misaligned. Even if you have a team of highly skilled individuals, if they're not aligned with the tasks at hand, the organization will suffer. It's like having talented soccer players on the field but not positioning them strategically – you'll end up with a game plan that falls apart."

CHAPTER FOUR: ALIGNMENT AND RE-ALIGNMENT

Ben inquires, "Do you occasionally transfer staff between positions to ensure alignment and realignment?"

John responds, "Actually, we aim to ensure that each employee is placed in their ideal role from the outset. Mastery of a role is crucial, and constant reassignment could impede this process. We strive for stability in our team placements to foster expertise and proficiency."

Ben asks, "Could you elaborate on what you mean by mastery of the job?"

John suggests, "Given our time constraints, I propose we reconvene tomorrow to continue our discussion. What are your thoughts on that, honorable?"

Ben responds, "Certainly, Director."

Chapter Five: Mastery of Jobs

While at home, Ben, as usual, finds himself lost in thought, reflecting on his encounter with John. His wife notices his distant demeanor during their conversation.

"Hey honey, are you with me? You seem lost in thought. Don't tell me you're still dwelling on your time at that company? Oh, and there's something I've been meaning to ask you. You haven't been going there alone, have you?"

"Indeed, I've been going there solo."

"Isn't it quite a load for you, dear? Why not bring along a couple of your directors? A firsthand experience could do wonders for them, don't you think? Plus, it might ease the weight of absorbing all that knowledge by yourself. It shouldn't feel like a one man show, after all."

"My dear wife, I truly commend you for pointing that out. It's a glaring oversight on my part, and I must admit, it leaves me feeling quite exposed and embarrassed."

"Honey, it wasn't my intention to make you feel that way. Sometimes, experiences come to light to reveal our shortcomings, urging us to improve. In the end, they turn out to be blessings in disguise."

"I truly feel blessed to have you as my wife. Instead of dwelling on embarrassment, I should see this as a blessing. It's an opportunity for me to grow and become a better person than I was yesterday."

"Indeed, my dear husband, as the saying goes, 'iron sharpens iron.'"

They both share a hearty laugh over the matter.

The next morning, Ben summons two of his directors to his office and recounts his recent visit to the Spencer Agro-processing Company Limited over the past couple of days. He urges them to join him on a visit to gain firsthand insight into the operations of this dynamic manufacturing enterprise. He elaborates on how the company embraces "management by harmony" as its operational ethos, emphasizing its significance in shaping the organization's current success. His intent in briefing them on this MBH management philosophy beforehand is to mentally prepare them for the upcoming tour.

Later on, Ben contacts the professor and shares the latest developments with him.

The professor responds, expressing his satisfaction with Ben's decision to involve his colleagues in the tour. He remarks that he would have been disappointed if Ben had gone alone through to the end of the program, but he's pleased that Ben didn't overlook the importance of teamwork.

Ben's response lacks enthusiasm, as he acknowledges that the initiative to include his colleagues stemmed from his wife rather than his own realization. Soon, the trio arrives at the manufacturing company's premises. They are warmly welcomed into the boardroom by the ever-smiling gentleman. Both the CEO and John join them, and in his opening remarks, Ben strategically outlines the agenda to make his directors feel involved and to mask his earlier oversight. To the professor and John, it seems as though the inclusion of the two directors was part of the original plan. The directors, introduced as Steve and Peter, are seamlessly integrated into the discussion. Ben recounts how he briefed them on the background of the management philosophy of harmony, as taught by the Professor.

Ben inquires about the concept of job mastery and its significance within the framework of the MBH philosophy.

John responds, emphasizing the critical importance of mastery in the MBH philosophy. He illustrates this concept using the analogy of a biological body, where each part must function effectively to maintain overall harmony. John stresses that just as every body part must master its assigned task for the body to function optimally, every employee must possess the necessary skills and expertise to perform their duties in an organization.

He warns against compromising on employee qualifications, as underqualified staff can lead to organizational underperformance and inefficiency, disrupting the harmony of the entire system. John vividly depicts how an unskilled employee can create a ripple effect of inefficiency and disharmony throughout the organization, highlighting the detrimental impact of incompetence on organizational performance.

Peter questions, seeking to understand how the organization ensures that its staff remain up-to-date with the constantly evolving landscape of skills and knowledge.

John replies, outlining the organization's commitment to transformational leadership, which focuses on unlocking the potential of employees rather than expecting them to arrive fully formed. He emphasizes their investment in training and development, citing the example of personnel currently abroad for training. Moreover, he highlights their emphasis on creativity and innovation, particularly within their research and development department, where over 90% of their recipes are locally generated.

John quotes Gallup Consultants, underscoring the importance of investing in employees' talents for organizational success. He describes their R&D department as "beyond the book," symbolizing the encouragement to surpass conventional boundaries in pursuit of innovation. Lastly, he explains their approach of fostering ownership of goals as a means to ensure mastery of jobs.

Chapter Six: Ownership of Goals

Ben queries about the importance of employees taking ownership of objectives to enhance organizational performance.

John passionately explains the profound significance of employees taking ownership of organizational objectives to enhance performance. He emphasizes that employee engagement is crucial for organizational success, quoting the insights of Gallup Consultants. Goals, he asserts, are the essence of any organization's existence, formulated by the board and communicated down the management hierarchy. However, many organizations fall short of optimal performance because employees are often mere recipients of goals, lacking ownership and involvement in their formulation.

John highlights the importance of employees feeling a sense of ownership towards organizational goals. When employees feel consulted and involved in goal-setting, it boosts their self-esteem and commitment. He stresses that wisdom and innovative ideas can emerge from any level of the organization, not just from leadership. Ultimately, aligning the initiatives of both employers and employees fosters a harmonious work environment where everyone is motivated to contribute to the organization's success.

CHAPTER SIX: OWNERSHIP OF GOALS

Peter's voice echoes with curiosity as he seeks clarification on how employees can actively participate in the setting of organizational goals.

John's response reverberates with a sense of urgency and passion as he delves into various avenues for employees to actively participate in goal setting. He emphasizes the importance of breaking away from rigidity and exclusivity in the formulation of goals, urging organizations to tap into the intellect of their employees, who are the ultimate implementers of these goals.

John advocates for a more inclusive approach, suggesting methods such as internal surveys and welcoming new employees' ideas for improvement from the outset of their engagement. He passionately critiques the common practice of neglecting to familiarize new employees with organizational goals during orientation, highlighting the detrimental impact on organizational performance. John's words carry a weighty urgency, challenging the status quo and calling for a paradigm shift towards harmony in goal formulation that incorporates employees' perspectives.

In a sudden twist, John then calls upon Cathy, the newest addition to the organization, inviting her to share her insights on the induction process, a move that signals a commitment to transparency and employee involvement in the organizational dialogue.

In strides a maiden of tender years, her countenance bearing the weight of anticipation walks in. With solemn ceremony, the director proclaims her arrival, yet she, in her quiet resolve, already discerns the purpose behind her summons, for it was ordained earlier before this moment.

John states that the team has convened with the specific intent of learning about your orientation journey.

Cathy initiates her narrative with a sense of humility in acknowledging the presence of the esteemed minister and his accompanying delegation. She expresses her enthusiasm in sharing her induction encounter within this organization, driven by her prior professional engagements spanning three different workplaces. The profound impact of her experience here has left her in awe. Contrary to her traditional understanding of orientation, shaped by past experiences, she found her introduction here to be a transformative departure from mere acquaintanceship with colleagues, particularly those she anticipated closely collaborating with.

"Alright, this piques my curiosity. Pray, do continue," Ben interjects, his interruption laced with anticipation.

Cathy proceeds with her narrative, explaining a prevalent concept within the organization known as "Baptism into Organizational Beliefs" (BIOB), a ritual conducted during the "Meet the CEO" program. She elaborates that new employees are expected to undergo this baptismal process, wherein the CEO imparts the organization's core beliefs during the orientation or induction phase.

"Hold on just a moment, madam!" Peter interjects with an air of urgency. "I catch two intriguing terms in your narrative: 'Meet the CEO' and 'baptism into organizational beliefs'. Enlighten us on their nature and their profound significance."

Cathy responds, expressing gratitude for the inquiry. She reveals that the "Meet the CEO" program is an obligatory component of the organization's orientation process, mandated for all new employees. During this session, new hires engage in a formal encounter with the CEO and pertinent directors, facilitating a substantive dialogue.

CHAPTER SIX: OWNERSHIP OF GOALS

The CEO, alongside the directors, expounds upon the organizational beliefs through thorough explanation and illustrative examples. Furthermore, a test is administered to gauge the employees' comprehension and application of these principles, colloquially termed as "baptism into organizational beliefs."

Moreover, the "Meet the CEO" session is instrumental in acquainting employees with the organizational objectives, delineating each goal individually and expounding its correlation with their respective roles. A thorough examination of job descriptions follows, allowing for clarifications through an open forum for inquiries.

In a moment of contemplation, Peter muses aloud, his tone tinged with curiosity and skepticism. "A valid point, madam. Numerous organizations articulate their goals and job descriptions within their advertisements. Why, then, is there a need to revisit these aspects during the 'Meet the CEO' session?"

Cathy responds, acknowledging Peter's point and offering a rationale for revisiting organizational goals and job descriptions during the "Meet the CEO" session. She contends that advertisements represent a unilateral form of communication, lacking the opportunity for applicants to seek clarification on any unclear aspects. Cathy asserts that many applicants may not have a comprehensive understanding of the objectives and job descriptions presented in advertisements, prompting the necessity for further clarification and elaboration during the orientation process.

"But wouldn't enlisted applicants have the chance to seek clarification during interviews?" Peter poses the question, his voice charged with skepticism and curiosity.

Cathy elaborates on the limitations of interviews as a platform for detailed conversations, highlighting the constraints posed by factors such as time, mood, and atmosphere. She emphasizes the missed opportunity for organizations to foster intellectual connection with new employees during orientation, which serves as a pivotal moment for laying the groundwork for robust employee engagement. Cathy observes that many employees, left to navigate their roles independently, may hesitate to seek clarification from supervisors, fearing a perception of incompetence.

Contrastingly, the unique atmosphere fostered during the "Meet the CEO" session in this organization facilitates open dialogue and intellectual engagement, enabling employees to develop a profound understanding of organizational goals and their role within the broader network.

This informal and friendly setting encourages uninhibited inquiry, fostering a sense of ownership over organizational objectives. Moreover, the immersion in organizational beliefs during this session cultivates alignment with the organizational culture, underlining the significance of a strong cultural foundation in organizational success.

Cathy asserts that the "Meet the CEO" experience instills employees with a sense of purpose and confidence from the outset, positioning them for success in their roles. Unlike in many organizations where the CEO may seem inaccessible, here, the CEO is approachable, further enhancing the employee experience.

"Gentlemen," Ben interjects, his voice resonating with conviction and authority, "I believe we can all resonate deeply with Cathy's insights. Drawing from my own experiences across multiple organizations, I wholeheartedly concur with her perspective. There's no doubt in my mind that her explanation encapsulates the dynamic essence of this organization. I've found myself in situations where I've had to navigate new roles without adequate guidance, and it's a scenario that's unfortunately all too common, despite being inherently abnormal."

Steve's bewilderment is palpable as he exclaims, "This is utterly astonishing! I've always viewed orientation as a mere formality for introductions. But this perspective is truly enlightening."

Peter chimes in, his tone reflective, "Indeed, from what we've heard, it seems that this level of engagement permeates the entire organization, evident in its remarkable success story."

John interjects with a sense of validation, "Your observation is astute, sir. In this organization, we place great emphasis on fostering strong and harmonious internal relationships. Allow me to propose that we address the agenda of nurturing these relationships further. However, before we delve into that matter, I extend an invitation to you, gentlemen, to join me on a visit to our manufacturing plant. There, you'll witness firsthand the amicable and welcoming environment that permeates our entire organization."

With a gracious nod towards Cathy for her valuable contribution to the discussion, John excuses her to resume her regular duties.

With a flourish of gratitude, Cathy bids farewell, "I extend my sincere thanks once more for this opportunity. It has truly been my pleasure."

Chapter Seven: Nurturing Internal Relationships

The four gentlemen emerge from the boardroom, traversing a walkway flanked by desolate stretches of parched grass, until they reach a state-of-the-art building situated approximately 100 meters from the Administration building. Stepping into the reception area, they are greeted with warm smiles from two young ladies. The receptionists' demeanor indicates an anticipation rather than surprise, suggesting they were prepared for the quartet's arrival at the manufacturing plant.

One of the receptionists promptly guides the gentlemen to the office of the plant manager, who wastes no time in ushering them into the heart of the plant. Inside, they are met with a scene of men and women clad in appropriate work attire, diligently operating various specialized machineries.

"Here's something I've noticed," Ben remarks with a sharp eye, "Your organizational motto, plastered in sticker form all around the plant."

John responds with a solemn nod, "Indeed, it serves as a constant reminder to each worker of our identity, values, and culture. We're committed to preserving our essence and principles, hence the imperative of these daily reminders in the form of stickers."

With the visitors granted free rein to interact with the workers, the trio eagerly engage in conversations. The workers, evidently honored by the opportunity to engage with such esteemed guests, readily share their thoughts and experiences. Spending nearly an hour mingling with the workers, the trio not only foster connections but also gather valuable feedback—a task John particularly embraces in his capacity as director for human resource and harmony.

Expressing gratitude to the plant manager, the four gentlemen make their way back to the boardroom. Once convened, they collectively realize that another day is warranted to fully explore their discussions. However, one unanimous conclusion emerges from their tour: the palpable sense of camaraderie and warmth among the workers. Their interactions reflect a familial bond, underscoring the friendly and cordial atmosphere that permeates the entire organization.

"Following my interviews with several workers about their seamless camaraderie," Ben reflects, "They unanimously revealed to me their deep-rooted embrace of the 'home away from home' culture—a foundational belief of this organization."

John responds with a resolute tone, "While our previous discussions have touched upon this topic, it's crucial to emphasize that 'home away from home' is a cornerstone belief shaping our organizational culture. As you know, every employee undergoes mandatory immersion into these beliefs during the 'Meet the CEO' experience of orientation."

Peter interjects with a sense of urgency, "During my inquiry about conflict resolution, one worker recounted how they are trained to swiftly escalate any conflict or potential discord to the plant manager. Without delay, the manager involves the harmony department if the matter proves too complex to resolve internally."

John responds with a profound statement, underlining the significance of fostering internal cohesion for optimal organizational performance. He asserts that the organizational atmosphere can either serve as a balm for emotional stress or exacerbate it, as it can cultivate either a nurturing environment of love and care or one fraught with intimidation and callousness. The diverse array of personalities, cultural backgrounds, and religious beliefs within an organization inherently heightens the likelihood of personality clashes and conflicts of interest, necessitating emotional intelligence and a comprehensive approach to creating a conducive atmosphere for all employees.

Acknowledging the dynamic nature of harmony within an organization, John emphasizes the need for a dedicated section to ensure the establishment and maintenance of both internal and external harmony. He stresses that organizational performance thrives in an environment of constant rapport, where both vertical (between employees and management) and horizontal (among employees themselves) relationships are characterized by mutual respect and friendliness. John highlights the detrimental impact of relational conflicts, which can impede organizational performance if left unchecked, often manifesting in actions that undermine and hinder each other's effectiveness.

Peter poses a pointed question, his voice carrying an air of intensity, "Beyond the specialized section dedicated to fostering harmony within the organization, what role does leadership play in cultivating this internal rapport?"

The top leadership within an organization holds a pivotal

CHAPTER SEVEN: NURTURING INTERNAL RELATIONSHIPS

role in determining its overall health and functionality. As the central governing system, management bears the significant responsibility of fostering a culture of positive rapport throughout the organization. Much like the central nervous system in the human body, a healthy management structure is essential for ensuring harmony among the various components of the organization. Just as any dysfunction in the nervous system can disrupt the entire body's functioning, disorganization at the top levels of leadership can lead to widespread disharmony and dysfunction within the organization.

The behavior and interactions of top leadership set the tone for the organization. Employees closely observe how their leaders engage with one another, and this sets a precedent for the atmosphere within the entire workforce. History has shown that nations have descended into civil unrest when government leaders fail to maintain a harmonious relationship amongst themselves, leading to division and animosity among their followers. This ripple effect is often magnified at lower levels of the organization, where employees may align themselves with certain factions within the leadership hierarchy.

Thus, it is imperative for organizations to prioritize the cultivation of internal rapport among their leadership team, as this sets the foundation upon which all other aspects of harmony within the organization are built. This principle should be deeply ingrained within the organizational culture, permeating every facet of its operations.

Ben expresses his gratitude to the director with a sense of earnestness, "Thank you, sir, for your thorough explanation. One other observation I've made is the steadfast commitment to your organization's deeply emphasized values and beliefs."

John responds with a tone of resonance, "Your insight is

sharp,"

and it leads us to the final point I wish to emphasize: 'yoked together.'"

Steve inquires with an air of intrigue, "And what, precisely, does that entail, sir?"

Chapter Eight: Yoked Together

John declares with conviction, "The concept of 'yoked together' embodies a harmonious alignment in shared values and behavioral norms. It fosters a unified sense of purpose and communication among organization members. Every organization upholds a set of values and behavioral standards outlined in its code of conduct manuals. These standards are paramount as they define and interpret the organization's culture, thereby shaping its public image. Moreover, the 'yoked together' principle facilitates corporate governance by establishing benchmarks for the behavior expected from organization members."

Ben poses his question with an edge of intensity, "What consequences do you anticipate from deviating or compromising on our values, beliefs, and code of conduct?"

John delves into the significance of upholding this crucial concept, highlighting how its disregard has led to the underperformance and eventual closure of numerous organizations. It typically begins with an erosion or compromise of the organization's values and behavioral standards. When an organization loses sight of its values, it embarks on a perilous path towards decline. The most severe consequence is when a single organization's compromise on good corporate governance has a ripple effect on the broader economy.

For instance, consider a local mining firm with international stakeholders that was implicated in tax evasion through financial manipulation, resulting in significant loss of tax revenue for the country. This case underscores how poor corporate governance not only impacts the organization itself but also its stakeholders, including government and society at large. The infamous Enron scandal of 2001 serves as another stark example, with its detrimental effects on thousands of individuals due to fiduciary breaches.

MBH's objective is to unify all organization members through adherence to shared values and behavioral standards. This entails not only alignment in values and behaviors but also in communication. Speech holds immense power and effectiveness, as seen in the ancient Tower of Babel story. When members of an organization speak in harmony, it signifies a unified and optimistic outlook on the organization's trajectory and performance. This principle, when embraced and upheld, yields positive results, while neglecting it results in negative repercussions for the organization.

In a moment of intrigue, Steve poses a question charged with intensity, "And how, precisely, do you enforce unwavering adherence to the values, beliefs, and code of conduct?"

John responds with a managerial approach, stating, "We ensure strict adherence to our values, beliefs, and code of conduct through continuous monitoring, detection, and control mechanisms. The responsibility for monitoring and addressing deviations from these standards, including financial irregularities and breaches of behavioral standards, lies with a dedicated Harmony Department. This independent unit is tasked with oversight to prevent compromises that may arise from conflicts of interest among officers directly or indirectly involved in the departments they audit. Each department is represented within this section by professionals."

Ben bids adieu with a profound sense of gratitude, "Gentlemen, our time together draws to a close. Allow me to express my sincere gratitude for your presence here today. It has truly been a pleasure to share this enlightening experience with you. Let us anticipate more moments like this in the future, as we embark on what I believe to be the first of many enriching encounters."

John concludes with a flourish, "It has been an honor to host you all here today, and I eagerly anticipate the prospect of many more such moments in the future. Thank you once again for your presence and participation."

With a sense of purpose, Ben and his colleagues depart the boardroom, making their way to the office of the CEO. As they enter, they are greeted by the esteemed figure of the CEO, who also holds the title of Professor, welcoming them warmly into his office.

The Professor extends a formal welcome, stating, "Gentlemen, I trust that your time here has been enriching, and I hope you depart with valuable insights that may prove beneficial to your ministry's endeavors."

Ben responds formally, expressing, "We are immensely grateful for this exceptional opportunity. It is undeniable, Professor, that your ubiquitous influence and visionary mindset are palpable throughout the entire organization and its workforce. In summary, what concise message do you have for us?"

The professor responds in a managerial tone, stating, "Certainly, honorable. As I recall, I previously emphasized the importance of balancing the welfare of the organization with that of its employees, highlighting that effective management leadership entails navigating the tradeoff between the two pursuits.

During our discussion on systematic thinking, I provided a detailed analogy using the human body to illustrate how stress can lead to various diseases and disorders. We are currently in an era marked by widespread stress, with employees being no exception as they are part of a stressed community beyond their roles within the organization.

Therefore, it is imperative for leadership to cultivate a stress-free environment and atmosphere for them. Displacement and dissatisfaction can contribute to a stressful environment, ultimately resulting in decreased performance within the organization. We consistently strive to prioritize the well-being of our employees to the best of our ability."

Peter's inquiry is imbued with a sense of drama as he asks, "Could you elaborate on what you mean by 'displacement' and 'dissatisfaction'?"

The professor delivers his fervent reply
, explaining, "Displacement occurs when employees are assigned to roles that do not align with their skill set, hindering their ability to perform effectively and efficiently. Often, we may mistakenly attribute underperformance to individual shortcomings, overlooking the possibility that employees are placed in roles that do not leverage their strengths.

This misalignment can lead to feelings of stress and frustration among employees. If we aim to expand their responsibilities beyond their current skill set, it is crucial to provide them with appropriate training and support.

Dissatisfaction arises when employees lack the enthusiasm and motivation to fulfill their duties due to inadequate working conditions or terms of employment. Employees should not perceive themselves solely as instruments for the organization's goals, but rather as valued individuals whose personal well-being matters. Leadership must prioritize the welfare of employees, which is why we place great emphasis on creating a 'home away from home' environment in our organization. Additionally, we embrace a strength-based management approach, which focuses on maximizing, building, and leveraging employees' strengths while mitigating weaknesses, rather than solely concentrating on addressing weaknesses."

Steve poses a question, "What, in your opinion, is the origin of stress?"

The professor responds with depth and urgency, "That's a pertinent and timely inquiry. Stress is triggered by a chemical release from the brain when the mind perceives the environment as threatening and beyond its control. This chemical suppresses the immune system and inhibits cell growth or replacement, as all energy is redirected towards the 'fight or flight' response.

Consequently, opportunistic diseases may arise due to the compromised immune system. The crux lies in mastering how to interpret the environment effectively. Here, we educate our employees on the art of subjectively interpreting their surroundings to their advantage. Every situation holds neither inherently good nor bad qualities until assigned meaning. Thus, we empower our employees to assign meanings that serve their interests.

The loss of control over a situation often stems from the interpretation attached to it. Our organization places significant emphasis on teaching stress management, overseen by our Harmony Department. Malfunctioning due to stress among employees can have detrimental effects on organizational performance. Management by harmony dictates that every facet of the organization operates in sync. Harmony should infuse every aspect of organizational behavior and performance."

Ben reflects, "What a remarkable way to wrap up our mission. Your concise summary perfectly captures the insights we've gained."

The professor responds graciously, "The honor is mine, esteemed guests. We look forward to future opportunities to convene in such enriching discussions. Gentlemen, thank you once more for accepting our invitation. Now, allow me the pleasure of seeing you off."

The professor accompanies them to the parking area, and the trio departs from the premises.

CHAPTER EIGHT: YOKED TOGETHER

CHECK LIST

Blurb

"Management by Harmony" introduces a groundbreaking approach to leadership that prioritizes synergy, collaboration, and balance in the workplace. Authored by GoodsonMumba, a visionary leader with a passion for harmonious management practices, this book offers a fresh perspective on how to inspire, motivate, and empower teams to achieve peak performance. Drawing on principles from Eastern philosophy, organizational psychology, and modern management theory, "Management by Harmony" presents practical strategies, real-world case studies, and transformative insights to help leaders cultivate a culture of harmony, trust, and mutual respect. Whether you're a seasoned executive or a budding manager, this book will revolutionize the way you think about leadership, fostering a more harmonious and productive work environment for everyone.

About the Author

Goodson Mumba is a multifaceted individual known for his diverse expertise and prolific contributions across various fields. As an infopreneur, Management Consultant, thought leader, and spiritual leader, he has inspired countless individuals through his insightful teachings and impactful writings. Mumba is also an accomplished author, with several notable works to his name, including "Understanding Corporate Worship," "The Years I Spent in a Week," "Management By Harmony," "The CEO's Diary," "Change to Change" and "Creative Thinking for results" His literary works span topics ranging from business management to personal development and spirituality, reflecting his broad range of interests and insights.

With a Master of Business Leadership (MBL) and a Bachelor of Arts in Theology (BTh), Mumba brings a unique blend of business acumen and spiritual wisdom to his work. His educational background is further enriched by a Group Diploma in Management Studies, providing him with a solid foundation in organizational dynamics and leadership principles. Additionally, Mumba holds diplomas in Education Psychology, Leadership and Management Styles, Organizational Behaviour, Financial Accounting, Economic Growth and Development, and Project Management, showcasing his commitment to continuous learning and professional development.

Mumba's expertise extends beyond traditional academic disciplines, encompassing areas such as Neuro-Linguistic Programming (NLP) and Positive Psychology. His diverse skill set is complemented by a range of certifications, including Creative Problem Solving and Decision Making, Life Coaching Fundamentals and Techniques, Professional Life Coaching, and Performance Management System Design. These certifications reflect Mumba's dedication to equipping himself with the tools and knowledge necessary to empower others and drive positive change.

As an author, Mumba's writings reflect his deep understanding of human nature, organizational dynamics, and spiritual principles. His works offer practical insights, actionable strategies, and inspirational guidance for individuals seeking personal growth, professional success, and spiritual fulfillment. Mumba's holistic approach to life and leadership resonates with readers worldwide, making him a respected figure in both the business and spiritual communities.

Overall, Goodson Mumba's diverse background, extensive knowledge, and profound insights make him a sought-after speaker, mentor, and author. His commitment to excellence, lifelong learning, and service to others continues to inspire individuals to unlock their full potential and lead lives of purpose and significance.

Goodson Mumba is renowned for initiating the concept of Management by Harmony, revolutionizing traditional management practices with a focus on balanced and holistic approaches. He has authored two influential books on this subject: "Introduction to Management by Harmony" and its sequel, "Management by Harmony."

Mumba's work has significantly impacted the field, offering innovative strategies for fostering organizational harmony and efficiency. His contributions continue to shape contemporary management theories and practices.

www.ingramcontent.com/pod-product-compliance
Lightning Source LLC
Chambersburg PA
CBHW070204230526
45471CB00002B/819